Mary E. Martin

THE LUMINOUS DISARRAY

5/99

Madeleine —
For another
lover of movement
and words —

Mary E. Martin

Floating Bowl Press

Acknowledgements
        Thanks to the editors of the following publications where some of
these poems were first pubiished: "Tableau" in *Cimarron Review*; "I could
waltz across Texas with you" in *Southern Poetry Review*; "A Handful of
Twigs" in *One Meadway*; "Meditation," "Hard Scrabble Pass,"
"The Candidate's Rally," "Southwestern Baroque," and "Idyll" in *Kansas
Quarterly*; "Last Light," "Note from a Dancer," "City Park," and "Running
with the Mountains" in *Calapooya Collage*; "The Lesson of Numbers" in *Fresh
Grounds*; "Grieving is Never Predictable" in *The Wisconsin Review*; "Village of
the Mermaids" in *West Branch*; "The Ohio Valley" in *Crazy River*; "The
Luminous Disarray," "Pushing Off," and "Shallow Water" in *The Charlotte
Poetry Review*; "An Organ-grinder's Farewell" in *Lactuca*; "Hymn # 28" in
Sow's Ear Review; "Return of the Light" in *The Soul's Labyrinth*; "Mirage" and
"The Dance Teacher" appears in *The Art and Craft of Poetry* by Michael J.
Bugeja.
        Many thanks to the those who inspired me to continue: Mitzi
Brown, Jonathan Holden, Jenny Brantley and Brian Fitch, Karma Smith,
Nancy Stover, Susan Warden, Susan Hunt, Jeffrey Luber, The Data Studio,
Alison Wheatley, Karen Steele, Bob DeMott, Linda Muir, Glenna Batson,
Colette Inez, Marilyn Atlas, Pearson Cross, Anna McDaniel, Cathy Smith
Bowers, Tom Andrews, Melissa Pope, Libby Patenaud, Laura Faure, Bob
Hayden, Leslie Bennett, Pat Deweese, Raj, Kathleen Reilly, Richard Rollison,
Steve and Nora Martin, Richard and Nadine Day, Kirsten Dabelko, Lanny
Flaherty, Jim and Kay Fuller, Carl and Deb Foster, Bill and Elaine Martin,
Jodie Glorioso, Jim Hancock and Suzan Zeder, Gloria Jones, Mary Kratt,
Elizabeth Marks, Paul Tuttle, Dick Goode, Nadia Moustafa, and a special
thanks to Kevin Bezner and Michael J. Bugeja.
        With love and gratitude to my family: my mother, Dorothy
O'Connor Martin, and my father, John D. Martin and his wife, Yvonne, and to
the clan— Pat and John Kuehn, Paula Powers, and Gary and Jackie Martin,
and all my nieces and nephews.

Martin, Mary E. , 1948-
The Luminous Disarray/ Mary E. Martin
ISBN 0-89002-339-5
Library of Congress Catalog Number: 98-071748

Floating Bowl Press   Produced in association with:
PO Box 31184   Northwood Press
Charlotte, North Carolina 28231-1184   Conservatory of
                                             American Letters
                                             PO Box 298
                                             Thomaston, Maine 04861

Contents

FOR MITZI, MICKEY, KARMA, AND KEVIN

I.

The Luminous Disarray

for Emile Snyder

What if the thin membrane
of the moon were blown away,
a yolk running into the stars, gathering
the constellations, filling
in their webbed forms, massing them
together until all our heroes
become one silver arrow heaved,
arcing out of the sky and roaring
toward us: we would be as still
as Pompeii, the silver air like lava
would catch us, rush through us,
and blinking we would stare,
confused at the brightness
of our breathing, how we move
like silk— then the luminous disarray,
feeling the pressure of light
no longer outside, but within us.

Tableau
for Jenny and Laura

It's spring and all that clung
to us in winter—the quilts, our clothes,
our lovers—has changed with the weather.
We sit in the backyard
pared down, watching the shrubs and trees fill out,
give us privacy. The stubble
of new grass shows more promise
than we do, but the sun helps, glazing
over our anxious skin, giving us
the glamorous tinge we need to lapse
into the embrace of summer—warm air
wrapping around us as we whisper
of the young men passing by.
Our bareness, so exactly
who we are, never changes.
Each spring we face what's left—
white flesh, the residue of cold
nights in our joints, the unveiling
of our posture—a blur of hope
no matter what.
We slumber on the lawn,
make nests of our dreams,
keep ourselves quiet enough
to let the birds fly close,
hear how loud their wings can be.

"I could waltz across Texas with you"

Of course I'm excited
when you ask me to move
the desert in three-four time.
It may be jerky, brambles
sticking to our clothes,
but our feet toughen with each measure
sweeping us further and smoother;
nothing can stop this momentum,
not even the burn
from our grasping turns,
the dizzy air of sun, or our panic
for a polka that wants to run past rhythm.
Air lifts, assumes our voices,
lost in steps, in the beveling
of our words, syllables curve
skyward from our pivoting bodies.
The slope of our phrases gives
shoulders to the moon;
and there we balance
the moon with our thoughts,
luminous, gliding horizontally, not knowing
when the prairie will end.

Walk in Late Fall

(for Diana Khoury, 1958-1983)

Flowers stiffened to relics,
air cloisters beneath
the arch of stone gray trees.
It's here, at the time
before hard-edged shadows
are scattered by snow
when I imagine your withered
body bruised, marrow
evaporating, still forcing
your fingers to draw a forest
minutely exposing a final bird.
There was nothing
of your tragedy in your sketch
of the goat-footed man,
his head flung
back with a flute, hair
twined with petals and sky.
The marvel of your secrecy—
it leaves me stunned.
Here, where my breath is ether
numbing all motion,
I would kneel,
give you my bones.

A Handful of Twigs

I keep hearing you read
your haikus, a handful of twigs
you gave to the lake,
the simple wood of the words
will float . . .
resting our bodies,
two unheard sounds on a blanket
listening to each other,
overwhelmed with the extremities
of water, two aimless fish,
scales reciting
the dryness of shore
until we're evenly passed
between the sun and water,
feeling the spread of sail
and your words,
small boats lingering.

The Ohio Valley
July, 1991
for Johanna and Jennifer

The dry hay little comfort
beneath our feet, hot haze
clamping us down under
the lean-to, we scan
our campsite, praying for rain,

but end up stripped and floating
in the pond, circling each other,
flesh happy, daring the hidden
sun to come closer. As we carve
the water, undulate from shape

to shape, we consecrate
what is below, the mud plush
between our toes, and above,
the bare white bowl of sky
where we imagine tossing

the pale pink blooms up
from the field, rose-of-Sharon;
the deep purple centers, sweet dark
stars, outlining our constellation—

three women unburied from the hot day,
from not knowing each other,
weaving garlands, our fingers
connected by the fringe of flowers,

and all around,
catching our breath, quick
flecks of hummingbirds.

Forgetting a Friend

Of course it's more
than our sleepless chatter I remember
sitting early mornings, limp and drifting
in the Café du Monde, New Orleans, watching
the sun crack over the river,
the startle of a warm day.
The sleek still freighters,
black dreams in water,
remind me of that night I'd caught
in your gaze a burst
jagged and quick like fire,
the danger vanishing as I sank
chilled in your embrace, closing
my eyes to cut the glance from your face.
And in our waking-to-sleep moments,
the cafe rousing, we watched those dark bodies
slowly glide out of harbor.

*

For seven years I followed you
out my back door . . .
Atlanta, Indiana,
wherever you dumped a six-pack,
spawned a few friends.
Your songs of affliction, your unsold art
inviting me cross-country, I always
stopped in. Whatever my arms caught
I accepted.
Once we lifted mattresses to the roof,
stalked the sky naked. We spoke invincibly
of survival at bars, talk that carved
stories in bar walls and doors.

*

Now through the dark body of the phone
your voice leaves each word
far away from where you are.
You say things change, and only my breath
responds, sensing your static return
to New Orleans, your giving in to home.
I stutter about dance,
the hard solo I do, trying
not to remember that jagged glance,
that weapon, your soul; only wanting
to recall the water, those mornings
we sat on the edge of the water, allowing
our shoulders to stretch back, opening
our ribs, pouring out to the waves below
all we ever had to offer.

Mirage

Suddenly there is motion in the desert.
Arms like scarves
signal me over out of the sun,
under the tent strewn with pillows,
plates of fruit and wine. As I stare
at the billowing walls I'm grabbed
by a man in armor who doesn't speak
but stretches his tongue out beyond
the grid of his helmet licking
each crevice, each turn my body takes.

He drapes me in white silk,
and I float from cushion to cushion
afraid to know where I am.
The billows become halls,
a continuous sway of space
where I wander, always the clatter
of his steps close by. I'm allowed to touch
nothing but him, feel nothing but him,
his silver hands, the chalice
from which I must drink.

Hymn #28

Let's sit together
on your couch.
I will begin
by baring one breast.
We will listen to the radio news,
comment while fondling each other
how extreme events seem to be.
It's not that the world
isn't nice, or that we
don't enjoy each other,
but we could be changed
forever. There is a danger
in allowing heaven
to enter our bodies.
The angels might squeeze
our breath in their ecstasy,
the saints in glorious rhythm
could march too heavy down our spines,
clouds would eventually saturate
our muscles, seep into our eyes.
We might find ourselves
so full of heaven
we couldn't sing,
or even stand to praise
the day we were born.

Pushing Off

Like Tennyson's Ulysses
I knew you would disappear.
The snow's restless arrival
didn't stop you when your bike
struck the road, *a hard
gem-like flame*, burning
into the country, the pinched
trees and weed whiskered land
still a place you claim as escape.

When there appeared no route
left toward any star,
you'd stop by offering
bitten pizza and beer,
enough belief
in danger to make any world new,
even in these last years
of the century; the close

touch of our breath, the tropical
pull of our bodies would navigate
beyond doubt. Curved against
your black leather jacket, your wide
maroon bike, we prized the wind,
aware what we both must do
is more than we'll ever
know of each other. What gives us
too much motion in soul and body
is not finding the end of the world,

but looking for a loosening
in the juncture of earth and sky,
distance quivering as we shift
toward what allows
us to survive, to surrender.

A Sense of Touch
for Ann

I.
We grew like damp crystals
in the summers of Mississippi
in the wild arms of honeysuckle
we bedded deeper each day.
The mud consumed us
moved us through the slow golden hair
of the rivers, the sun's rhythm
in the forest, of heat
waving from pavement.
It was hard to untie
our dreams from the ribbons
that kept our flesh wet and sinking.

Always we listened
to the early evening drift of harps,
captured at the edge of the porch,
sweet shadows
blowing in our ears
the subtle darkness.

II.
Half the days in Utah
we would sit drinking coffee
pouring out
all our warm illusions,
a sense of touch.

Your cough
shook the snow as we smoked and walked
against the wind, barely surviving
the search for jobs,
the nervous businessmen,
their eyes like ants
all over us,
the snow turning
us white
we dragged ourselves
like bundles of beggar's clothes.
The cold hands of buildings
wouldn't feed us.

We felt extravagant at night,
leaving bars drunk
and loving
the close bonds made
by lovers who passed between us.

III.
Look at us now:
we have a history.
Across the country
you live in a bottle of snow,
your eyelashes frozen, your body blank
from believing you will be fulfilled,
your pale shape fired
like a furnace, suddenly blasted with joy.

Each day I begin to dance
I must locate
another limb, try to attach it,
force the muscle to brace
me higher than before.
Each day I awake
dismembered.

When you call we press ourselves
back against the skull,
the rough hug of bone
reviving our voices.

Possibilities

for Allison

I've heard that in the fields
of India, maybe Africa,
women simply squat
to labor, their new babies dropping,
squealing onto the hot ground—
a break from the chores of planting.
And here we are so curious
about what fills us,
recording first movements,
describing crazy dreams,
the budding convex of our bodies.

I watch you like spring,
curious if I could
mimic what most women can do,
succumbing to our great epic,
the rhythm larger
than pleasure, where we descend
and rise in the same moment,
gripping down
into the final deep
push, propelling the head out,
suspending until the first breath
rattles through tiny wet lips.

So at six months you sit
encircled by your unborn;
I'm charmed
as if the air were swarmed
by little feet and hands
kicking for attention; I am drawn
to the promise of children,
but these possibilities
settle like lost colonies
once I maneuver back
to my cave of words, to the sweep
of my body in dance where I carry
myself too far before returning.

Already your baby
is older than I imagine.

II.

Meditation

In winter waking, star-prints
left on windows, you breathe
slowly, dress quickly,
quietly leave your cabin, walking
into the forest as into a den
of crystals, columns, and sky,
where each step tells
the pressure the snow takes
beneath you, a sharp
yet gentle echo of reply;
the snow is full of light
and brings you past
what you think is a morning
walk, to a sensation
infinite as a prism,
a clarity of warmth
for all you know of the world,
for anyone whose effect
you remember, while the white
branches tumble above,
and every color possible
hitting, finds your heart.

The Lesson of Numbers

Columbus, Georgia

I always scurried from clocks,
knew nothing of minutes,
only sensations, burrowing
my feet into the land of red clay,
whizzing my bike down the road
that cut and dipped through the swamp,
free from the ticking
and blank rubbing of numbers.

There were nights my mother
pushed and pushed
matchsticks across our formica-topped
dining table, forcing me
to add and subtract, her quick fingers
collecting, bundling, straightening them,
and I noticing only the designs,
the space between the matchsticks.

In the fourth grade after stuttering
before the clock, the teacher,
the class, I shrugged red-faced
and sat for training.
I forged numbers on my tablet,
shouted divisions at my parents,
slung decimals against glass,
and when I ran into the forest
out back of our house
I would quietly crouch
in pine needles and grass,
my folded arms
bare and straining as I hummed
and puffed my breath.

Shallow Water

I've never breathed well
in water, my lungs
have stuttered and clutched
ever since high school—
the swim coach, her blue-white hair
bobbing with each whistle
she blew as we lined
up to the diving board, and I
skinny and long as the boys,
shivering, the tight squeeze
of my bathing cap marking my fear.

The lessons still with me,
now lyrical equals
among a group of dancers
rushing for a swim,
I watch them slide into the lake,
smooth ribbons trailing their strokes,
and randomly stop
hushed in waist-high water
before surface diving.
I watch as the curves
of their stretched feet,
those flawless shells, briefly extend
into air before disappearing.

I plunge into the water, feel my feet
kick free to air, sputtering wild blades
arching me the wrong way, and I clench,
shove against the water to reverse
my bend, my shoulder jutting out
as I rise. Wading back
to shore, cradling my arm,
I couldn't tell them
how much I hurt myself, how little
it took to lose grace with the world,
a minor lapse of rhythm,
leaving only a wrinkle of a wave
as the lake engulfed my shy history.

Last Light
the "Widow" Combs in Appalachia

In a scarf sustaining
a wafer of face, color pinched
from her eyes, the old woman
wishes to be the rock
she's crouched on, to be the unnoticed
land, where her fingers
have dug, where she has places to rest,
the ground an eternity beneath her.
She knows machines will arrive,
hack her acres apart, steel gullets
will eat her trees to their spines, gorge down
deep beyond water, leaving holes
for hell to drop in.

*

But she raises herself, stands
before their hulking shovels
by the roots of her muscles,
demanding retreat, standing
long hours with a crippled stick,
then lying down before them.
She shivers and whispers
to the dirt, rolling slightly
side to side, enough to curve
herself in the earth, cupping her hands
as if rain were falling right to them.

*

Summoned, the sheriff, his men
arrive and cleave her from the mountain,
pick her up like a rock,
lifting her from each end
down the road, rudely silent
while she sinks in cold air.
She has lost the sense of her bones
and cannot feel their grip

cannot feel the knot of the scarf
rubbing dirt under her chin.
In the wind her body flutters,
buckles like a sagging angel.

The Candidate's Rally

Thunder louder than the jammed
brick streets, the politician's speech
sinks past the swirl of heads and necks
as I jut my umbrella tip against
the butts of beer-jeering students.
But their shouts are drowned as the marching band
bursts like locomotive steam—it thrills me,
as if this is what we all believe in,
all gasping in awe of the lone baton above us,

its gratifying twinkle like an odd prize
secretly cherished, a gift we either took
or received, most of us too young—
I was, in junior high after a dissecting frenzy,
wrapping the delicate pink and blue starfish,
a rubbery formaldehyde limp, running
down the street with my treasure.
No one but me knew the inside of this star,
a pleasure impossible to explain until now,

the baton twirling above me catches it,
a free-floating quest that fires us
beyond our glib biology,
our crowding together to gawk
at some faceless messenger,
and the clouds, dark and restless,
about to shake us down.

The Palace of Illusions
at the Cabarrus County Fair

The electric Woman, the Six
Legged Cow, the Exorcist Girl,
The Man Who Bleeds continuously—
all played against the fabric
of the circus tent coarse enough
to cloud their movements,
but this man, the only real show;
his dyed black hair could rub
off like charcoal onto his bare beige
suit, and when he speaks
his eyes sink deeper back,
his hoarse throat the sooty cave
leading to his leathered bellows
that each night fans then eats
the fire, the magic
a mere hazard,
but it is the sword, how he bends
forward as the silver blade pries
back and forth beyond his mouth
before it slides as far as it can go,
and always the mythic retrieval—
the wet blade emerges
virginal from his gut,
a victory for the whole group
of freaks whose illusions
couldn't stand such inward
challenge, who looks
to this man as their leader,
their host of every show
performed in every small county,
this wizened automatic swallower
still proving to the crowds
his worth, the precious
length of his Adam's apple
a valued curse.

Holy Cards

Finally I paste a gold
glitter halo around my head,
just like I did when twelve
around pictures of prettier
girls, priests, Jesus,
Mary, especially pained
saints. Now I too have feet
that touch the globe
without injury to fish, flesh
or foul, without the pitter-patter
of running away to hide my toenails.
I blaze among the sunflowers,
my skirt the mediterranean blue
sway at noontide; I can catch
a fall or spill with it, rumble
the gutter grates as I clap
hosannahs in the streets.

I laminate new holy cards—
my mother proud behind her four
children and her hand sewn Easter dresses,
or my father with sunglasses
in the driver's seat,
his back turned to us all;
one family, two holy cards.

I sleep with my gold halo
still on, my holy cards
under the pillow, prayers flying in
through the open window.

Running with the Mountains

Watch for snakes:
they love to bake in the sun.
So you run, the valley so perfectly
poised, your eyes grazing
the asphalt for anything coiled,
long or lazy while you listen
for the roar of trucks or jeeps
until a car sneaks up and you jump
fearing you've landed on a rattler,
but your breathing keeps
control as you recover stride
and springing forward the whole road
empties for you, your body stretching
to all that's ahead: the fields of cattle
and fence clustered around
barns and homes, the space between
each giving them a place
you won't forget, how they all
move or stay together—the cows,
the fence, the wind, the homes,
and to one side, how the mountains
never stop.

City Park

My dog seeks
this brave square of land
everyday. While he jousts
and counters the multitude of smells
I follow, swinging
the banner of his leash.
Only a schnauzer would offer
the imperative to any dog
he meets. I am careful
to restrain his chivalry.
In this mystical place
of picnics and sports we rove,
fiercely questing the right
moment to drop honor
onto the ground.

An Organ-grinder's Farewell

Moving shifts your guts around.
You begin to like being
empty; the street appears
a comfort as you stroll between
dinners and cafes, from friend
to friend, each parting a jumble
of hands and eyes leaving one
last imprint, leaving you
cranking out good-byes
to anyone passing by;
you wave to Albert, the organ-grinder
stooped by the local deli,
his grey beard dangling.
He asks you to go with him to grieve
at Luigi's casket—his last monkey
dead. You stay and dance
to the organ, taunting
Albert to play. Some days the music
trickles like melted sugar,
your feet lightly brushing
the concrete, other days the music
pummels the street with loud fists
while you dodge the angry money.
Tired of the neighborhood you follow
Albert from corner to corner, mile
by mile, he playing, you dancing, down
the highways, at rest stops,
entertaining truckers for a meal.
You cut his beard, he washes
your bandanna, but it's too hot,
the pavement burns, so you search
for country roads, settling
beneath a canopy of trees,
the organ pelting into silence,
your feet soothed by the grass.

And it's here you both discover
not moving, how miraculous
your farewell has been,
slow scallops of sound and motion
edging far from the city
toward this simple space.

III.

Southwestern Baroque

It isn't paradise, but the patrons
of this Santa Fe cafe appreciate
the swish of my skirt table to table,
a counterpoint to the fickle cussing
of the counter regulars, the sharp
yells from the cooks, the smothered
chiles rellenos bulging
hot seeds in tourists' mouths,
and the sensual, yet calculated singing
of the Mexican kitchen help
lusting after that blond waitress
makes sense of the red pepper
sauce splattered all over
the pick-up station.
If I am to be broke
what better place,
polishing silver napkin holders,
sudsing the hidden filigree
of drink machines, watching
Indians crown ornate birds
with colored ink as I pour
their coffee.
This could be
as opulent as Rubens, as precise
as the vaulted sound of Bach,
a place to prophesy
beyond all that falling.

Epistle to Thackery

Yes, I have thought of myself
as that sea monster roiling
beneath the water, that Becky Sharp
who is all beauty and cunning
from the waist up, but below
the waist she is out of control,
explosive, a corpulent mass
of scales and barnacles, a vivid
display of sin. I see my duality
everyday, standing before
my students, the swish
of that lethal tail disrupting
my thoughts, causing me
to shift my weight frequently
behind my brown corduroy skirt,
or addressing my lover,
my whole body tilting
side to side from the bulging
weight of my sin.

But let me tell you,
I'm not clever like Becky;
I'm simply plagued with the weight.
Dragging the burden
of my reptilian body, water edging
just under my ribs, breasts drifting
atop, I try to smile
serenely because I'm afraid at any
moment the serpent
will take over, claw
my face into a snarl, hiss my hair
just like Medussa's,
and I will be left with the debris,
empty wrappers, my shed skin floating
all around me. Not even Amelia
would recognize me; no continent

would accept me. I would be left to roam
the deserts of ice in either direction,
the rash of cold winds unfurling
my brittle, moody tail.

Note from a Dancer

Diving behind our skin we forget
most people pay nothing
to move, but sometimes we feel odd
just walking, aware of the length of our spine,
how much we mend and replace muscle
with thought. When dancing we value
how motion utters certainties
most people don't speak.
Our necks are costly
in the time it takes to circle
out the sleep of winter mornings.
Our backs must be open, always expanding
to what we can't see;
our shoulders willingly must confirm
the constant voyage of our arms.
Even the space around us
becomes irreplaceable
the instant we begin to move.

But last night we performed in a restaurant,
dancing too close to tables.
We did it for exposure,
the customers smiling, their eyes pricing
dance as cheap, dirt cheap.

Black Place III

after a painting by Georgia O'Keeffe

Hard earth slows
my fall as I press
myself towards the opening,

skidding past
rock, down through dust-blind
air to the desert below.

Then the landing,
shadowless, the small light
from my eyes not enough.

I unbend, stumble tight
and grey, wade with dim
legs through sand

towards a moment which dissolves,
inhaling a light
I've never known.

Where birds slip through clouds,
I continue their decline—
where wings fall to haze

then darkness, there is a place
where white falls through

and the lily opens, petals thundering
as I drop down the damp black stem.

The Dance Teacher

The community has seen you thrown
around a man's shoulders, then slung
to his feet smiling, your back
arched, feet pointed, sometimes a shadow
of graceful passion behind
the scrim, other times performed
center stage, his fingers
noticeably pressed into your waist,
your thighs in the light.
Each concert it works
for jazz, ballet,
or modern—the pas de deux
the man, always a new student
who can't move well yet, but
sturdy as a tree trunk,
lifts you, whirls you,
circles the stage with you
above him, your fingers
fanned in bravura, legs
starched in a kick back,
your neck muscles propping up
your grin, just as the fog rolls in
from the wings and the girls
waltz on, laced with garlands
of plastic flowers, surrounding
you like an altar.
This is what you're known for,
to be light enough to be tossed
around on stage, a few moments
of being handled and the audience
squirms and ahhhs! and little girls
with sticky fingers suddenly
want to dance watching you up there,
pretending to be a swan,
a mermaid, a fountainhead, a spout,
a chronic fixture.

Village of the Mermaids

after a painting by Paul Delvaux

In the distance the long curl
of their bodies on the beach,
close to the moon white mountains.
But in the village the mermaids
sit in long dresses, colors
muted like their hands
firm as marble on still laps,
the empty street marked
by their figures beside each door,
their hair turning in the same
gold wave, waiting for lovers
who have clothed and placed them,

promising the world.
Cotton gowns fit loosely
except where the bodice presses
around their breasts, as the bare
mountains press against the village,
the one street nudging through
the row of rooms to the beach,
each room large enough
a space for the tangling
of two bodies, his two
legs rippling like her fin.

Afterwards the men escape
quietly down the street, confident
they've captured the enchantment,
but thinking what has never been
felt in their lives before
is not much different.
Occasionally at night, rubbing up
against their wives, the men
wail in their sleep
as if pleading the sea to bring them
a storm, a cloud
of stark and whirling arms.

The Art Barge

Montauk, Long Island

More an ark waiting
for a gust in the water,
I stroll the decks, peering in
the silent rooms rowed
with easels and mud-smeared tables
ready for a change in weather.

Leaning on the rail, restless
as this sandy perch, I close my eyes,
imagine the rumble
of footsteps, people quickly filling
the rooms, their fingers
and eyes hard at work in the light, aided
by the rhythm of water beside them.

Their gestures merging, each dip
for paint, each pat on clay would arc
like the cluster of dancers
gliding, their torsos tuned
to musicians roaming the aisles.
None would mind borrowing
in such reverie. One back
might turn for a curve
in sound, another soar
for a spiral whip of paint.
Words in silence become colors,
dialogue, an epiphany of light,
the air a gauze so sheer
even flecks of sand on the floor
wouldn't be hidden but openly
charged with beauty.

The rising storm would not distract them,
the black sky unable to bruise their focus.
Even when the ocean bashed
the barge wouldn't crack,

they would know they were safe in the ribs
of the ark. They would float and sway
as long as it took to finish their work,
to bring life back,
an offer gently pressed.

Marina Dancing

"The Eye sees more than the heart knows"
—Blake

Sad zigzag of the body,
I watch your pliant
grieving, muscular
as Blake's etchings,
your quick twist
to run, lost as Albion's
daughters trapped
in the cave of the stage,
or the country of the audience.
Yet no clouds turned flames
turned rainbows arc above,
just you in a blue sack dress;
your limbs, so elemental
in their weight and time,
give us the vision that has
rent many of us asunder.

As each move thickens
the space, leaving veil
upon veil, the invisible
sound of your body
pushing away the air,
you forward all loss—
my mother, her friend,
your motion, our myth.
I watch how you simply
sit on a high stool, music
stopped, and press your hand
straight before us, slowly
smoothing down a scar
we can't see.

Idyll

Balanced on the top
floor of the parking garage,
open to the sky for fifty five
cents an hour, the late fall
heightening the trees' cross-hatching
of neighborhoods and hills,
I tower between two steeples,
wavering above the low whistling
cars, where pigeons peck the air.
Distance so literal, the town so visible,
I fidget, steady myself to see further. . .
the momentary rise reminds me
how the mind rests
like a folded swan, assured
of beauty in the ascent, wing-span
spreading past my eyes, past
the panorama, where my breath briefly
chisels a gem from the clouds;
the power in the return not a lament
but in the wheels winding to the street,
beneath the tires, I hear the grace,
the ordinary grit spin and pop.

IV.

Return of the Light
December, 1985

In the hospital the glare of sun
above the mountains is welcomed.
I do not shield my eyes. I imagine
how many friends in the nearby
mountain valley where my parents live
have gathered, lifting
my sick mother with their arms
overhead towards the clouds, then throwing
her up to the light,
catching her
just in time to throw her
up again. No one tires,
their palms resilient as souls
tossing her up
until her body clear as light
no longer aches, until her pain has dropped
to the ground rusted
and trampled beneath the people
propelled by their own nimbleness
and her weightless descending, until all arms
in unison gently let her down.
She looks around brushing her gown
then mingles with her friends,
her head briskly turning
the blue from her eyes more alive
now than when
she first felt love.

Two Men Toast Before Dinner

Dad offers Earl a slug
of bourbon. They both shift
their weight,
affirming where they are,
their wives desperate with cancer.
His cowboy shirt holding
in his guts, Earl spews out
he's alcoholic, *but don't tell her
I'm drinking—her head's full
of lumps.* Earl drains out
more about his family, his daughter's
black boyfriend, *the color of your shoes,*
looking at my father's feet. My father laughs,
suddenly forgetting about his wife,
the weariness of watching
the spoon lift to her mouth,
and remembers world war II when blacks
were niggers who played softball—Earl coughs
for another drink. Dad quietly
gives more, the two men toast
the evening, Earl saying he doesn't care
the man's nice to my daughter,
my father, pushing his shoulders back,
well, their blood's as red as our's.
Their eyes slowly circle out
trying to define the horizon,
discover why a winter evening
is so warm.

Corresponding

This winter you write me
speaking of your father's bad
heart; I reply, detailing
my mother's cancer,
how the distance from her
gives me nightmares, feeling
her shaking, with his needle
the doctor unable to find
her liver—at least you're home
to see how sore his breathing is.
Two weeks later you assure me
home is no better,
how seeing him everyday is a constant
budge towards death, how each morning
you must find a new way to brighten
his room; how the flowers suffocate.

The more the illness comes, the less
there is to say. I'm traveling
home more; you hardly leave the house.
But the letters keep arriving.
I stack them by the phone.
Thin and weightless
they lie like bodies stacked
tightly, but more compressed,
frail as lungs collapsed.

At My Mother's Side

If ever I could be a dark figure
in the middle of the night, I was then,
running across
the empty street, darting
through the street lamps' rigid
skirts of light to meet
the hospital coldly before me, worse
than any shadow from behind.
I rushed in panting
before the elevator, just in time
slipping past the doors.
Bloated and barely breathing,
you lay cloaked with secrets,
your eyes already closed.
At first I stood, then sat by you, walked
the hall slowly, the sickness
from each room intensely quiet,
yet clicking. I held your hand
as it turned blue,
refused to wipe the red foam from your mouth,
kept kissing your forehead
as if I had the right
to offer blessing.
Finally I receded from the room
out into the morning,
feeling guilty at what
had been stolen in the night,
what would be stolen again.

For Dorothy Martin, 1922-1986

The air is warm and gentle
like a story told to comfort.
Balancing high on the ladder
I fill myself with mulberries, linger
for the small clump of plump buds
to fall and hit me,
splash me in a flurry of leaves
jostling with birds, my fingers
splotched dark red, juice staining
my tongue; I close my eyes
and wait for nothing
to reply. But my lips respond
by luring what is deep
to rise, the reverse of rain
in a whisper; unspoken words
for my mother quietly
refill the tree.

The words cling
in ripe clusters, scrawl along
the limbs, crowd the leaves;
birds peck at the new
sweet fruit that sounds
in their throats as they fly.
I listen to all I've ever wished
my mother to hear,
the space between branches
echoing to a shimmer in my ears.
As I open my eyes I lean
against the trunk, press
close to the bark, the heart
of all that circles and continues.

Hard Scrabble Pass

Custer County, Colorado

Nosing up the pass in the foggy
October chill, I expect the road
to be slippery, the rock gray,
my mother's house still
as when she died. But as I round
the sudden curve
slabs of mountainside push
orange and red from their crevices,
smudge blue where rock
juts out from shadow;
the aspen leaves gold
as the air is wet.
Even the green is lush
like mink around the bright
cold streams. My urge to move,
to sway among the trees and colors
is given over to the car
as it slowly swings up the pass.
Then tilting with the road the car
plunges into the valley,
the glide down to Westcliffe
time enough to settle
all doubts about the journey,
to know it's never
hard to be here, in the lilt
of a valley that carries me
so vibrantly from land to house,
from night to day.

The Mother and Daughter Banquet
April, 1988

The ceiling low
as in all church basements,
pink crepe flowers puff
from pillars that interrupt
rows of cafeteria tables,
the off-white curtains closed
over windows level with the lawn.
And all of us sit
level and straight,
three hundred women and girls

each of us facing
a wedge of angel food doused
in orange sauce. If my mother
were here she would worry
about the lipstick on her teeth
when she smiled, breathe deep
to keep her back from slumping.

Many receive prizes of geraniums,
begonias for their prodigious
flock; the great grandmothers
blush behind their flowers
as we nod and fork our bright
orange cake. My mother would be happy
to complain, and yes, I wish
I could hear her nag again
how I'm not married, her eldest,
a good girl who's wasted time.

Chatter would shuffle
over tables until my awkward,
watery gaze would be caught
by someone sniffling,
almost gurgling like an ancient bird
from a table across the room—
it would be Miss Havisham
in her crippled way complaining too,

slowly rising, weeds of old lace
hanging from her arms, declaring
how she never married either,

her body jerking with each step
down the aisle, how she's all
alone with Estella's cold heart
far away, the women shoving
their chairs away, mice pattering
from beneath her shredded
gown, children darting everywhere.
She pauses at the end of the row,
her fine hair waving like smoke,
looking for her table,
the marriage banquet still set,
and cries to be back
at Satis House—no one moves,

a stench like old wounds
scares them, they've never seen
a woman so barren. I nudge my mother
to close her gaping mouth,
breathe calmly, be ready,
for Miss Havisham
with even the remnants of her passion
could set the room afire.

Grieving is Never Predictable

for Jenny

I.

What happened
we would ask,
couched on a riverbank,
to those love affairs
where it was okay
to light candles
and over-react?
Nothing had to work out.
Now we barely
make a pass; we've lost
our touch, we chant,
our fingers tugging
at new grass, our bodies
curled in shade, beneath us
the blanket veined by tiny ants
while we sip and brood, champagne
bottles swishing down
a small Kansas river.

II.

I hear you shudder
over the phone, your grandmother
dead. Go, dig a small hole
by your side; reach in, rub the damp
earth between your fingers
like a soft rosary,
roll each bead long enough,
know how dark peace can be—
more than a veil covering your eyes
it is a blanket around the spine, inclining
your gestures to find relief.
Roll each bead long enough
until you slowly repair
yourself, patting the dirt
back in, then bending a twig

or fixing a stone so you can return
whenever you wake stranded,
your palm curling
around the dark, allowing
your fingers to stretch and retract,
then press the soil again.

III.
Once I pressed my head against
my mother's shaded chest.
She squinted, young and
settled in an Austrian
meadow, her arms relaxed
around my starched sun dress,
my five year old heart face
shy while she smiled
and rested, her slender
pale leg half-stretched,
sandal foot flexed
as if she might
have been rocking me
slightly just before
my father snapped
the picture. Staring at it now
I return to the slant of small body
cushioning deeper in her shadow,
her breathing rhythm enough
to sink beyond the light,
beyond her life, a chant
of rolling and unfolding.